Warcraft®: The Sunwell Trilogy™ Vol. 1
Written by Richard Knaak
Illustrated by Jae-Hwan Kim

Lettering and Layout - Rob Steen
Copy Editor - Peter Ahlstrom
Production Artists - James Lee and James Dashiell
Artist Liaison - Eddie Yu and Studio Ice
Cover Art - Vuduberi
Cover Design - Raymond Makowski

Editors - Rob Tokar and Jake Forbes
Digital Imaging Manager - Chris Buford
Pre-Press Manager - Antonio DePietro
Production Managers - Jennifer Miller and Mutsumi Miyazaki
Art Director - Matt Alford
Managing Editor - Jill Freshney
Editorial Director - Jeremy Ross
VP of Production - Ron Klamert
Editor-in-Chief - Mike Kiley
President and C.O.O. - John Parker
Publisher and C.E.O. - Stuart Levy

A **TOKYOPOP®** Manga

TOKYOPOP Inc.
5900 Wilshire Blvd. Suite 2000
Los Angeles, CA 90036

E-mail: info@TOKYOPOP.com
Come visit us online at www.TOKYOPOP.com

Special thanks to Chris Metzen and Elaine Di Iorio for their effort, energy, and enthusiasm.

ISBN: 1-59532-712-6

First TOKYOPOP printing: March 2005
10 9 8 7 6 5 4 3 2 1
Printed in the USA

VOLUME 1
DRAGON HUNT

WRITTEN BY
RICHARD KNAAK

ILLUSTRATED BY
JAE-HWAN KIM

HAMBURG // LONDON // LOS ANGELES // TOKYO

History of the World of Warcraft

No one knows exactly how the universe began, but it is clear that the Titans--a race of powerful, metal-skinned gods from the far reaches of the cosmos--explored the newborn universe and made it their mission to bring stability to the various worlds and ensure a safe future for the beings that would follow in their footsteps.

As part of their unfathomable, far-sighted plan to create order out of chaos, the Titans shaped the worlds by raising mighty mountains, dredging out vast seas, breathing skies and raging atmospheres into being, and empowering primitive races to maintain their reshaped worlds.

Ruled by an elite sect known as the Pantheon, the Titans brought order to a hundred million worlds scattered throughout the Great Dark Beyond during the first ages of creation. The benevolent Pantheon assigned their greatest warrior, Sargeras, to be the first line of defense against the extra-dimensional demonic beings of the Twisting Nether who sought only to destroy life and devour the energies of the living universe. Sargeras was more than powerful enough to defeat any and all threats he faced…except one.

Unfortunately for the Pantheon, the Titans' inability to conceive of evil or wickedness in any form worked against Sargeras. After countless millennia of witnessing the atrocities of the demonic beings he fought, Sargeras eventually fell into a state of deep confusion, despair and madness.

Sargeras lost all faith in his mission and the Titans' vision of an ordered universe. It wasn't long before he came to believe that the concept of order itself was folly, and that chaos and depravity were the only absolutes within the dark, lonely universe. Believing that the Titans themselves were responsible for creation's failure, Sargeras resolved to form an unstoppable army that would undo the Titans' works throughout the universe and set reality aflame.

Even Sargeras' titanic form became distorted from the corruption that plagued his once-noble heart. His eyes, hair, and beard erupted in fire, and his metallic bronze skin split open to reveal an endless furnace of blistering hate.

In his fury, Sargeras freed the loathsome demons he'd previously imprisoned. These cunning creatures bowed before the dark Titan's vast rage and offered to serve him in whatever malicious ways they could. From the ranks of the powerful Eredar, Sargeras picked two champions to command his demonic army of destruction. Kil'jaeden the Deceiver was chosen to seek out the darkest races in the universe and recruit them into Sargeras' ranks. The second champion, Archimonde the Defiler, was chosen to lead Sargeras' vast armies into battle against any who might resist the twisted Titan's will.

Once Sargeras saw that his armies were amassed and ready to follow his every command, he dubbed them the Burning Legion and launched them into the vastness of the Great Dark. To this date, it is still unclear how many worlds they ravaged on their unholy Burning Crusade across the universe.

Unaware of Sargeras' mission to undo their countless works, the Titans continued to move from world to world, shaping and ordering each planet as they saw fit. Along their journey, they happened upon a small world whose inhabitants would later name Azeroth.

For many ages, the Titans moved and shaped the soil, until at last there remained one perfect continent. At the continent's center, the Titans crafted a lake of scintillating energies. The lake, which they named the Well of Eternity, was to be the fount of life for the world. Its potent energies would nurture the bones of the world and empower life to take root in the land's rich soil. Over time, plants, trees, monsters, and creatures of every kind began to thrive on the primordial continent. As twilight fell on the final day of their labors, the Titans named the continent Kalimdor: "land of eternal starlight."

Satisfied that the small world had been ordered and that their work was done, the Titans prepared to leave Azeroth. However, before they departed, they charged the greatest species of the world with the task of watching over Kalimdor, lest any force should threaten its perfect tranquility. In that age, there were many dragonflights, yet there were five groups that held dominion over their brethren. It was these five flights that the Titans chose to shepherd the budding world. The greatest members of the Pantheon imbued a portion of their power upon each of the flights' leaders. These chosen majestic dragons became known as the Great Aspects, or the Dragon Aspects.

Empowered by the Pantheon, the Five Aspects were charged with the world's defense in the Titans' absence. With the dragons prepared to safeguard their creation, the Titans left Azeroth behind forever. Unfortunately, it was only a matter of time before Sargeras learned of the newborn world's existence.

In time, a primitive tribe of nocturnal humanoids cautiously made their way to the edges of the mesmerizing enchanted lake. Drawn by the Well's strange energies, the feral, nomadic humanoids built crude homes upon its tranquil shores. Over time, the Well's cosmic power affected the tribe, making them strong, wise, and virtually immortal. The tribe adopted the name Kaldorei, which meant "children of the stars" in their native tongue. To celebrate their budding society, they constructed great structures and temples around the lake's periphery.

The Kaldorei--or night elves, as they would later be known--worshipped the moon goddess, Elune, and believed that she slept within the Well's shimmering depths during the daylight hours. The early night elf priests and seers studied the Well with an insatiable curiosity, driven to plumb its untold secrets and power.

As the seemingly endless ages passed, the night elves' civilization expanded and Azshara, the night elves' beautiful and gifted queen, built an immense, wondrous palace on the Well's shore that housed her favored servitors within its bejewelled halls. Her servitors, whom she called the Quel'dorei or "Highborne", doted on her every command and believed themselves to be greater than the rest of their brethren.

Sharing the priests' curiosity towards the Well of Eternity, Azshara ordered the Highborne to plumb its secrets and reveal its true purpose in the world. The Highborne buried themselves in their work and studied the Well ceaselessly. In time, they developed the ability to manipulate and control the Well's cosmic energies. As their experiments progressed, the Highborne found that they could use their newfound powers to either create or destroy at their leisure. The heedless Highborne had stumbled upon primitive magic and they devoted themselves to its mastery.

The Highborne's reckless use of magic sent ripples of energy spiraling out from the Well of Eternity and into the Great Dark Beyond, where they were felt by Sargeras, the Great Enemy of all life. Spying the primordial world of Azeroth and sensing the limitless energies of the Well of Eternity, Sargeras resolved to destroy the fledgling world and claim its energies as his own.

Gathering his vast Burning Legion, Sargeras made his way towards the unsuspecting world of Azeroth. The Legion was composed of a million screaming demons, all ripped from the far corners of the universe, and the demons hungered for conquest.

Corrupted by the magics they wielded, Queen Azshara and the Highborne opened a vast, swirling portal within the depths of the Well of Eternity for Sargeras and his forces. The warrior-demons of the Burning Legion stormed into the world through the Well of Eternity, leaving only ash and sorrow in their wake. Though the brave Kaldorei warriors rushed to defend their ancient homeland, they were forced to give ground, inch by inch, before the fury of the Legion's onslaught.

When the dragons, led by the great red leviathan, Alexstrasza, sent their mighty flights to engage the demons and their infernal masters, all-out warfare erupted. As the battle raged across the burning fields of Kalimdor, a terrible turn of events unfolded. The details of the event have been lost to time, but it is known that Neltharion, the Dragon Aspect of the Earth, went mad during a critical engagement against the Burning Legion. He began to split apart as flame and rage erupted from his dark hide. Renaming himself Deathwing, the burning dragon turned on his brethren and drove the five dragonflights from the field of battle.

Deathwing's sudden betrayal was so destructive that the five dragonflights never truly recovered. Wounded and shocked,

Alexstrasza and the other noble dragons were forced to abandon their mortal allies.

Hatching a desperate plot to destroy the Well of Eternity, a band of Kaldorei freedom fighters clashed with the Highborne at the Well's edge. The ensuing battle threw the Highborne's carefully crafted spellwork into chaos, destabilizing the vortex within the Well and igniting a catastrophic chain of events that forever sundered the world. A massive explosion from the Well shattered the earth and blotted out the skies.

As the aftershocks from the Well's implosion rattled the bones of the world, the seas rushed in to fill the gaping wound left in the earth. Nearly eighty percent of Kalimdor's landmass had been blasted apart, leaving only a handful of separate continents surrounding the new, raging sea. At the center of the new sea, where the Well of Eternity once stood, was a tumultuous storm of tidal fury and chaotic energies. This terrible scar, known as the Maelstrom, would never cease its furious spinning. It would remain a constant reminder of the terrible catastrophe...and the utopian era that had been lost forever.

The few night elves that survived the horrific explosion rallied together on crudely made rafts and slowly made their way to the only landmass in sight. As they journeyed in silence, they surveyed the wreckage of their world and realized that their passions had wrought the destruction all around them. Though Sargeras and his Legion had been ripped from the world by the Well's destruction, the Kaldorei were left to ponder the terrible cost of victory.

Despite the devastation, there were many Highborne who survived the cataclysm--and who wanted to continue using magic. One had even stolen some waters of the Well of Eternity and created a new Well in the night elves' new homeland. Unable to come to terms with their fellow elves, the Highborne, or Quel'dorei, as Azshara had named them in ages past, set out on their own, eventually making their way to the eastern land men would call Lordaeron. They built their own magical kingdom, Quel'Thalas, and rejected the night elves' precepts of moon worship and nocturnal activity. Forever after, they would embrace the sun and be known only as the high elves.

Effectively cut off from the life-giving energies of the Well of Eternity, the high elves discovered that they were no longer immortal or immune to the elements. They also shrank somewhat in height, and their skin lost its characteristic violet hue. Despite their hardships, they encountered many wondrous creatures that had never been seen in Kalimdor…including humans.

Over the course of several thousand years, the high elves developed their society and made alliances with their neighboring human communities. Though the elves had constructed a series of monolithic Runestones at various points around Quel'Thalas to mask their magic from extra-dimensional threats, the humans who had learned magic from the elves were not so cautious. The sinister agents of the Burning Legion, who had been banished when the Well of Eternity collapsed, were lured back into the world by the heedless spellcasting of the human magicians of the city of Dalaran.

Under Sargeras' orders, the cunning demonlord Kil'jaeden plotted the Burning Legion's second invasion of Azeroth. Kil'jaeden surmised that he needed a new force to weaken Azeroth's defenses before the Legion even set foot upon the world. If the mortal races, such as the night elves and dragons, were forced to contend with a new threat, they would be too weak to pose any real resistance when the Legion's true invasion arrived.

Kil'jaeden discovered the lush world of Draenor floating peacefully within the Great Dark Beyond. Home to the shamanistic, clan-based orcs, Draenor was as idyllic as it was vast. Kil'jaeden knew that the noble orc clans had great potential to serve the Burning Legion if they could be cultivated properly.

Enthralling the elder orc shaman, Ner'zhul, in much the same way that Sargeras brought Queen Azshara under his control in ages past, the demon spread battle lust and savagery throughout the orc clans. Before long, the spiritual race was transformed into a bloodthirsty people.

Consumed with the curse of this new bloodlust, the orcs became the Burning Legion's greatest weapon. With the aid of a corrupted human mage, a Dark Portal was opened between Draenor and Azeroth, igniting an all-consuming war between the orcs and the humans. Though the human knights of Azeroth found allies in the high elves, the dwarves, and other species, the orcish ogres found allies in trolls, goblins, and more. Many human cities were utterly devastated and the orcs were poised to win the war until they fell victim to their own internal power struggles.

Seizing the opportunity, the humans retook their world and even fought the orcs in Draenor, though many heroic humans lost their lives when Draenor tore itself apart.

Though Ner'zhul was one of the many orcs who escaped Draenor's destruction, the orc shaman's body was torn apart by demons and his spirit was held helpless in stasis by Kil'jaeden. Recklessly agreeing to serve the demon, Ner'zhul's spirit was placed within a specially crafted block of diamond-hard ice gathered from the far reaches of the Twisting Nether. Encased within the frozen cask, Ner'zhul felt his consciousness expand ten thousand-fold. Warped by the demon's chaotic powers, Ner'zhul became a spectral being of unfathomable power. At that moment, the orc known as Ner'zhul was shattered forever, and the Lich King was born.

The Lich King was to spread a plague of death and terror across Azeroth that would snuff out human civilization forever. All those who died from the dreaded plague would arise as the undead, and their spirits would be bound to Ner'zhul's iron will forever.

Though the Lich King fought for the total eradication of human-kind, the wealthy and prestigious archmage, Kel'Thuzad, left the city of Dalaran to serve the evil creature. As the ranks of the undead swept across Lordaeron, King Terenas' only son, Prince Arthas, took up the fight against the Scourge. Arthas succeeded in killing Kel'Thuzad, but even so, the undead ranks swelled with every soldier that fell defending the land. Frustrated and stymied by the seemingly unstoppable enemy, Arthas took increasingly extreme steps to conquer them. Finally Arthas' comrades warned him that he was losing his hold on his humanity.

Arthas' fear and resolve proved to be his ultimate undoing. Believing that it would save his people, Arthas took up the cursed runeblade, Frostmourne. Though the sword did grant him unfathomable power, it also stole his soul and transformed him into the greatest of the Lich King's death knights. With his soul cast aside and his sanity shattered, Arthas led the Scourge against his own kingdom. Ultimately, Arthas murdered his own father, King Terenas, and crushed Lordaeron under the Lich King's iron heel.

Not long after Arthas and his army of the dead swept across the land, Kel'Thuzad was resurrected and not one living elf remained in Quel'Thalas. The glorious homeland of the high elves, which had stood for more than nine thousand years, was no more. Arthas subsequently led the Scourge south to Dalaran, and then to Kalimdor.

At Kalimdor, the night elves braced themselves and fought the Burning Legion with grim determination. Allied with humans and the orcs (now freed of their savage bloodlust), the night elves severed the Legion's anchor to the Well of Eternity. Unable to draw power from the Well itself, the Burning Legion began to crumble under the combined might of the mortal armies.

By this time, the undead Scourge had essentially transformed Lordaeron and Quel'Thalas into the toxic Plaguelands. The high elves grieved for the loss of their homeland and decided to call themselves blood elves in honor of their fallen people.

Meanwhile, half of the undead forces staged a coup for control over the undead empire. Eventually, the banshee Sylvanas Windrunner and her rebel undead--known as the Forsaken--claimed the ruined capital city of Lordaeron as their own and vowed to drive the Scourge and Kel'Thuzad from the land.

Though weakened, Arthas outmaneuvered the enemy forces that were closing in on the Lich King. Donning Ner'Zhul's unimaginably powerful helm, Arthas' spirit fused with Ner'zhul's to form a single mighty being--the new Lich King--and Arthas became one of the most powerful entities the world had ever known.

Currently, Arthas, the new and immortal Lich King, resides in Northrend; he is rumored to be rebuilding the citadel of Icecrown. His trusted lieutenant, Kel'Thuzad, commands the Scourge in the Plaguelands. Sylvanas and her rebel Forsaken hold only the Tirisfal Glades, a small portion of the war-torn kingdom, while the humans, orcs, and night elves are trying to rebuild their societies on Kalimdor.

AFTER WHAT SEEMED LIKE AGES OF BLOODY CONFLICT, THE WORLD THOUGHT IT HAD AT LAST FOUND PEACE. THE WAR AGAINST THE BRUTISH ORCS HAD COME TO A DEFINITIVE CONCLUSION, AND THE REMNANTS OF THE HORDE HAD BEEN ROUNDED INTO ENCLAVES AND KEPT UNDER GUARD.

SOON AFTER THE LANDS STARTED REBUILDING, A NEW, MONSTROUS EVIL AROSE. THE DEMONIC ARMY OF THE BURNING LEGION, UNITED WITH THE GHOULISH UNDEAD SCOURGE, SWEPT OVER HUMAN AND ORC REALMS ALIKE, FORCING OLD ENEMIES TO BAND TOGETHER.

YET, NOT UNTIL THE COMING OF THE MYSTERIOUS NIGHT ELVES AND THE SACRIFICE OF COUNTLESS LIVES WAS THE BURNING LEGION CRUSHED. NEARLY ALL OF THE ELVEN KINGDOM OF QUEL'THALAS AND THE HUMAN KINGDOM OF LORDAERON LAY IN RUINS, TRANSFORMED INTO FOUL PLAGUELANDS BY THE SCOURGE.

NOW, AN UNSTEADY STALEMATE EXISTS BETWEEN LIVING AND UNDEAD, AND FORCES FROM BOTH SIDES SEEK OUT THAT WHICH WILL DECISIVELY TIP THE SCALES IN THEIR FAVOR.

THUS IS IT THAT A YOUNG BLUE DRAGON WINGS HIS WAY TOWARD WHAT LITTLE REMAINS OF SOUTHERN LORDAERON...

DRAGON HUNT

NNNGH...

WE DON'T KNOW WHAT HAPPENED, BUT A HUGE EXPLOSION RIPPED THE AREA.

INSTEAD OF GAINING ITS POWER, THE ELVEN TRAITOR APPEARED TO SIMPLY DESTROY THE SUNWELL...

...OR SO WE THOUGHT...UNTIL RECENTLY.

CHAPTER TWO PURSUED

CHAPTER FOUR
LEGACY OF THE SUNWELL

IT WAS THE ESSENCE OF OUR LIVES...

...THE SOURCE OF THE MAGIC THAT WAS AS MUCH A PART OF US AS BREATHING OR EATING.

BUT FOR ALL THE GLORIES CREATED THROUGH THE SUNWELL...

...THE REWARD FOR MY PART IN IT WAS **NOTHING**.

SO I BEGAN SEEKING TO REWARD MYSELF FOR MY GOOD WORK.

NOT EXACTLY AN ELVEN NOTION, YOU MUST UNDERSTAND.

ARTHAS' GLORIOUS LEGIONS ATTACKED QUEL'THALAS, SLIPPING PAST ITS FABLED DEFENSES WITH MY AID.

MEANWHILE, HE HAD TAUGHT ME THE SPELL OF UNBINDING AND BINDING...

...AND STEELED MY NERVE WHEN I SET THE PLAN INTO MOTION.

THE VIOLENCE WAS REGRETTABLE...

...BUT SOME SACRIFICES MUST BE MADE FOR THE GREATER GOOD, YOU UNDERSTAND.

I COULD FEEL MY BLESSED LORD ARTHAS URGING ME ON!

I EVEN SENSED HIM USING HIS OWN MAGIC TO DRAW FORTH THE SUNWELL'S POWER...

...BETTER ENABLING ME TO ABSORB ALL OF IT, OF COURSE.

BUT THERE WERE THOSE WHO REFUSED TO ALLOW ME MY DUE!

THEY DARED TO CAST THEIR OWN SPELL IN THE MIDST OF MY GLORY!

THEY DARED TO TAKE MY SUNWELL FROM ME!

I FOUGHT THEM, MY BLESSED LORD AIDING ME WITH HIS MIGHTY STRENGTH...

...AND THEN, SOMETHING WENT TERRIBLY WRONG.

SOMETHING TORE THE SUNWELL'S POWER FROM MY GRIP! THE DESTRUCTION RAVAGED WHAT LITTLE REMAINED UNTOUCHED BY THE SCOURGE...

BUT I CARED NOT. I HAD SHAMED MYSELF BEFORE MY BLESSED LORD.

YET HE SAVED ME, AND SENT ME ACROSS THE CONTINENT...

...TO SEEK OUT WHERE THE SUNWELL'S MAGIC HAD GONE!

AND NOW... AFTER SO LONG...I SENSE IT IS NEAR...

NOTHING! NO ONE HERE HAS EVEN *HEARD* OF THIS *BOREL!*

I AM SORRY, KALEC!

To be continued in

Volume 2

The action heats up in the frigid wastelands as Kalec, Anveena, Tyri, and Jorad make their way to Aerie Peak.

They go seeking the dwarf known as Loggi, but they find much, much more.

As more fantastic and frightening denizens of the world of Warcraft are revealed, the mystery of Raac deepens and the dragons face a frozen and furious foe!

Can't wait for Volume 2? Go to tokyopop.com and check out our online manga player for some see sneak peeks at what's to come!

ABOUT THE CREATORS

In addition to his work on *Warcraft: The Sunwell Trilogy* and *Ragnarok* (also by TOKYOPOP), Richard A. Knaak is the NY Times bestselling fantasy author of 27 novels and over a dozen short pieces, including *The Legend of Huma* and *Night of Blood* for Dragonlance and *The Demon Soul* for Warcraft. He has also written the popular Dragonrealm series and several independent pieces. His works have been published in several languages, most recently Russian, Turkish, Bulgarian, Chinese, Czech, German, and Spanish. In addition to *Warcraft: The Sunwell Trilogy*, he is at work on *The Sundering*, the third volume of *War of the Ancients*, and *Empire of Blood*, the final book in his epic Dragonlance trilogy, *The Minotaur Wars*. All are due out in 2005.

Future works include a third Diablo novel and the *Aquilonia* trilogy, based on the worlds of Robert E. Howard. His most recent hardcover, *Tides of Blood,* the sequel to *Night,* was just released by Wizards of the Coast.

To find out more about Richard Knaak's projects or to sign up for his e-mail announcements, visit his website at http://www.sff.net/people/knaak

Jae-Hwan Kim was born in 1971 in Korea. His best-known manga works include *Rainbow*, *Combat Metal HeMoSoo*, and *King Of Hell* (called *Majeh* in Korea), an ongoing series currently published by TOKYOPOP. Jae-Hwan currently lives and works in Thailand.

NO. I'D RATHER KILL RATS.

Enter the World of Warcraft® and join thousands of mighty heroes in an online world of myth, magic and legendary adventure. Jagged snowy peaks, mountain fortresses, harsh winding canyons. Zeppelins flying over smoldering battlefields, epic sieges: an infinity of experiences await. Will you fight rats? No. Will you have fun? Yes, m'Lord. We didn't hold anything back in creating the World of Warcraft®. And now there's nothing holding you back. Visit www.worldofwarcraft.com today for more information. A world awaits...

WORLD OF WARCRAFT

MASSIVELY EPIC ONLINE

The savior of a world without hope faces her greatest challenge: Cleavage!

SOKORA REFUGEES™

Kana thought life couldn't get any worse—behind on her schoolwork and out of luck with boys, she is also the only one of her friends who hasn't "blossomed." When she falls through a magical portal in the girls' shower, she's transported to the enchanted world of Sokora—wearing nothing but a small robe! Now, on top of landing in this mysterious setting, she finds that her body is beginning to go through some tremendous changes.

Preview the manga at:
www.TOKYOPOP.com/sokora

BY SANTA INOUE

TOKYO TRIBES

Tokyo Tribes first hit Japanese audiences in the sleek pages of the ultra-hip skater fashion magazine *Boon.* Santa Inoue's hard-hitting tale of Tokyo street gangs battling it out in the concrete sprawl of Japan's capital raises the manga storytelling bar. Ornate with hip-hop trappings and packed with gangland grit, *Tokyo Tribes* paints a vivid, somewhat surreal vision of urban youth: rival gangs from various Tokyo barrios clash over turf, and when the heat between two of the tribes gets personal, a bitter rivalry explodes into all-out warfare.

~Luis Reyes, Editor

BY CLAMP

LEGAL DRUG

CLAMP is the four-woman studio famous for creating much of the world's most popular manga. For the past 15 years they have produced such hits as the adorable *Cardcaptor Sakura,* the dark and brooding *Tokyo Babylon,* and the sci-fi romantic comedy *Chobits.* In *Legal Drug,* we meet Kazahaya and Rikuou, two ordinary pharmacists who moonlight as amateur sleuths for a mysterious boss. *Legal Drug* is a perfect dose of mystery, psychic powers and the kind of homoerotic tension for which CLAMP is renowned.

~Lillian Diaz-Przybyl, Jr. Editor

BY MITSUKAZU MIHARA

DOLL

Mitsukazu Mihara's haunting *Doll* uses beautiful androids to examine what it means to be truly human. While the characters in *Doll* are draped in the chic Gothic-Lolita fashions that made Mihara-sensei famous, the themes explored are more universal—all emotions and walks of life have their day in *Doll*. *Doll* begins as a series of 'one-shot' stories and gradually dovetails into an epic of emotion and intrigue. It's like the *Twilight Zone* meets *Blade Runner!*

~Rob Tokar, Senior Editor

BY MAKOTO YUKIMURA

PLANETES

Makoto Yukimura's profoundly moving and graphically arresting *Planetes* posits a near future where mankind's colonization of space has begun. Young Hachimaki yearns to join this exciting new frontier. Instead, he cleans the glut of orbital junk mankind's initial foray into space produced. He works with Fee, a nicoline-addict beauty with an abrasive edge, and Yuri, a veteran spaceman with a tragic past in search of inner peace. *Planetes* combines the scope of Jules Verne (*Around the World in Eighty Days*) and Robert Heinlein (*Starship Troopers*) with the philosophical wonder of *2001: A Space Odyssey.*

~Luis Reyes, Editor

HYPER POLICE
BY MEE

In a future rife with crime, humans are an endangered species—and monsters have taken over! Natsuki is a cat girl who uses magical powers to enforce the law. However, her greatest threat doesn't come from the criminals. Her partner Sakura, a "nine-tailed" fox, plots to eat Natsuki and gobble up her magic! In this dog-eat-dog world, Natsuki fights to stay on top!

© MEE

LAGOON ENGINE
BY YUKIRU SUGISAKI

From the best-selling creator of *D·N·Angel!*

Yen and Jin are brothers in elementary school—and successors in the Ragun family craft. They are Gakushi, those who battle ghosts and evil spirits known as "Maga" by guessing their true name. As Yen and Jin train to join the family business, the two boys must keep their identities a secret...or risk death!

© Yukiru SUGISAKI

PhD: PHANTASY DEGREE
BY HEE-JOON SON

Sang is a fearlessly spunky young girl who is about to receive one hell of an education...at the Demon School Hades! She's on a mission to enroll into the monsters-only class. However, monster matriculation is not what is truly on her mind—she wants to acquire the fabled "King's Ring" from the fiancée of the chief commander of hell!

© SON HEE-JOON, DAIWON C.I. Inc.